D1231191

the power
of
mindfulness

Nyanaponika Thera

Unity Press

**MINDFULNESS
SERIES**

3

Copyright © 1972 by Unity Press

Published by Unity Press
PO Box 26350, San Francisco, Calif. 94126

Manufactured in the United States of America
ISBN No. 0-913300-02-0

First Printing 5000, August 1972

Introduction

This is a commentary on the Satipatthana mindfulness meditation, an inquiry into the scope of bare attention and the principal sources of its strength. Satipatthana, or the practice of mindfulness, was recommended by the Buddha for all who seek to grow spiritually and eventually attain the realization of enlightenment. Buddhism itself is essentially a practical path, a system of physical and psychological techniques designed to bring about this realization. The method here described is the foundation of all Buddhist meditation practice. It is, however, not necessary for you to be a Buddhist in order to practice mindfulness. It does not matter whether you are a Christian, a Jew, or an atheist, as the purpose here is simply to expand your consciousness and bring you face to face with your mind.

Buddhist psychology or Abhidharma teaches that you are not your mind. You already know that you are not your body. But you do not yet know that you are not your mind, because normally you identify yourself with each thought, feelings, impulse, emotion or sensation that comes into your mind. Each takes you on a little trip. Through the practice of mindfulness, you come to observe the rise and fall, the appearance and disappearance of these various thoughts and feelings, and gradually develop a sense of distance and detachment from them. Then you will no longer become caught by your hangups. This leads to a deep inner peaceful calm.

This book was offered to Unity Press for American publication by the Buddhist Publishing Society of Ceylon. A non-profit organization dedicated to spreading the timeless Teachings of the Buddha to all corners of the globe. Established in 1958 to promote knowledge of the Dharma, the Buddhist Publishing Society's publications are circulated in seventy-two countries. Nyanaponika Thera is the editor of the Buddhist Publishing Society, an authority of high repute whose many books have appeared in several languages. The best known of which is perhaps THE HEART OF BUDDHIST MEDITATION published in London by Rider and Company and available through the American distributor Samuel Weiser, a thorough guide to the vast applications of mindfulness, containing a rich anthology of ancient texts related to the subject.

Many of the technical Buddhist terms were capitalized in the original edition. We have for the purpose of clarity, and in an attempt to break abstraction, discarded the use of capitalizations which seem only to academicize the very real aspects of mind, (making nouns proper nouns, is like making things super things, out of context, attracting attention without expanding meaning, often misleading) perhaps creating in the reader, study, rather than absorption of the essence of the material. Where a common Buddhist term has been retained, we have put it in the more familiar Sanscrit, (which appears in dictionaries of English) rather than in Pali. For example, Dharma rather than Dhamma, as karma for kamma, arhat for arahat, nirvana for nibbana.

The Buddha was perhaps the greatest psychologist ever to have lived. The outcome of his investigations into mind are of immense value to anyone wishing to know himself. The Satipatthana investigations offer insight into the workings of mind, allowing us by application of bare attention, to come to the center, to watch, and to at last become free.

UNITY PRESS
1972

THE POWER OF MINDFULNESS

Is mindfulness actually a power in its own right as claimed by the title of this essay? Seen from the viewpoint of the ordinary purposes of life it does not seem so. From that angle, mindfulness, or attention, has a rather modest place among the many, and seemingly more important, mental faculties that serve the purposes of variegated wish-fulfillment. There, mindfulness means just "to watch one's steps" so that one may not stumble or miss a chance in the pursuit of one's aims. Only in the case of specific tasks and skills mindfulness is sometimes cultivated more deliberately, but here too it is still regarded as a subservient function, and its wider scope and possibilities are not recognized.

Even if one turns to the Buddha's doctrine, taking only a surface view of the various classifications and lists of mental factors in which mindfulness appears, one may be inclined to regard this faculty as just "one among many," and may get the impression that here too it has a rather subordinate place and is easily surpassed in significance by other faculties.

Mindfulness, in fact, has, if we may personify it, a rather unassuming character. Compared with it, mental factors like devotion, energy, imagination or intelligence are certainly "more colorful personalities," making an immediate and strong impact on people and situations. Their conquests are sometimes rapid and vast, though often insecure. Mindfulness, on the other hand, is of an unobtrusive nature. Its virtues shine inwardly, and in ordinary life most of its merits are passed on to other mental faculties, which receive generally all the credit. One must know it well and cultivate its acquaintance before one can appreciate the value and the silent penetrative influence of mindfulness. Mindfulness walks slowly and deliberately, and its daily task is of a rather humdrum nature. Yet, where it places its feet it cannot easily be dislodged, and it acquires and bestows true mastery of the ground it covers.

Mental faculties of such a nature are, like actual personalities of a similar type, often overlooked or underrated. In the case of mindfulness it required a genius like the Buddha to discover the "hidden talent" in the modest garb and to develop the vast inherent power of that potent seed. It is, indeed, the mark of a genius to perceive, and to harness, the power of the seemingly small. Here, truly, it happens that "what is little becomes much." A revaluation of values takes place. The standards of greatness and smallness change. Through the master mind of the Buddha, mindfulness is finally revealed as the Archimedean point from where the vast revolving mass of world suffering is levered out of its twofold anchorage in ignorance and craving.

The Buddha spoke of the power of mindfulness in a very emphatic way:

"Mindfulness, I declare, is all-helpful."

"All things can be mastered by mindfulness."

And further, that solemn and weighty utterance opening and concluding the *Satipatthāna Sutra*, the Discourse on the foundations of mindfulness:

This is the only way, monks, for the purification of beings, for the overcoming of sorrow and lamentation, for the destruction of pain and grief, for reaching the right path, for the attainment of *nirvana*, namely the four foundations of mindfulness.

Bare Attention

If, in ordinary life, mindfulness, or attention, is directed to any object, it is rarely sustained long enough for the purpose of factual observation. Generally, it is followed immediately by emotional reaction, discriminative thought, reflection, purposeful action. Also, in life and thought governed by the *dharma*, mindfulness *(sati)* is mostly linked with clear comprehension *(sampajanna)* of the right purpose, of reality. But for tapping the actual and potential *power* of mindfulness it is necessary to understand and deliberately cultivate it in its basic, unalloyed form, which we shall call *bare attention.*

By bare attention we understand the clear and single-minded awareness of what actually happens *to* us and *in* us, at the successive moments of perception. It is called "bare" because it attends to the bare facts of a perception without reacting to them by deed, speech, or mental comment. Ordinarily, that purely receptive state of mind is, as we have remarked, just a brief phase of the thought process of which one is often scarcely aware. But in the methodical development of mindfulness, aiming at the unfolding of its latent powers, bare attention is sustained for as long a time as one's strength of concentration permits. Bare attention is the key to the meditative practice of *satipatthāna,* opening the door to mind's mastery and final liberation.

Bare attention is developed in two ways: (1) as a methodical meditative practice with selected objects; (2) applied, as far as practicable, to the normal events of the day, together with a general attitude of mindfulness and clear comprehension. The details of the practice have been described elsewhere, and need not be repeated here.

The purpose of these pages is, in the first instance, to meet any doubts as to the efficacy of this method, i.e., as to the actual power of mindfulness. Particularly in an age like ours, with its superstitious worship of ceaseless external activity, there will be those who ask: "How can such a passive attitude of mind as that of bare attention possibly lead to the great results claimed for it?" In reply, one may be inclined to suggest to the questioner not to rely on the words of others, but to put those assertions of the Buddha to the test of personal experience. But those who do not yet know the Buddha's teaching well enough to accept it as a reliable guide may hesitate to take up, without good reasons, a practice that, just on account of its radical simplicity, may appear strange to them. In the following, a number of such "good reasons" are therefore proffered for the reader's scrutiny. They are also meant as introduction into the general spirit of *satipatthāna* and as pointers to its wide and significant perspectives. Furthermore, it is hoped that he who has taken up the methodical training will recognize in the following observations certain features of his own practice and be stimulated in their deliberate cultivation.

Four Sources of Power in Bare Attention

We shall now deal with four aspects of bare attention which are the mainsprings of the power of mindfulness. They are not the only sources of its strength but they are the principal ones to which the efficacy of this method of mental development is due. These four are:

1. the functions of "tidying up" and "naming" exercised by bare attention;
2. its nonviolent, noncoercive procedure;
3. the capacity of stopping and slowing down;
4. the directness of vision bestowed by bare attention.

Tidying up the mental household

If anyone whose mind is not harmonized and controlled through methodical meditative training should take a close look at his own everyday thoughts and activities, he will meet with a rather disconcerting sight. Apart from the few main channels of his purposeful thoughts and activities, he will everywhere be faced with a tangled mass of perceptions, thoughts, feelings, casual bodily movements, etc., showing a disorderliness and confusion which he would certainly not tolerate, e.g., in his living room. Yet this is the state of affairs that he takes for granted within a considerable portion of his waking life and normal mental activity. Let us now look at the details of that rather untidy picture.

First we meet a vast number of casual sense impressions, sights, and sounds that pass constantly through our mind. Most of them remain vague and fragmentary, and some are even based on faulty perceptions or misjudgments. Carrying these inherent weaknesses, they often form the untested basis for judgments and decisions on a higher level of consciousness. True, all these casual impressions need not and cannot be objects of focused attention. A stone on our road that happens to meet our glance will have a claim on our attention only if it obstructs our progress or is of interest to us for any other reason. Yet, if we neglect too much these casual impressions, we may stumble over many an actual, or figurative, stone, and overlook many a gem lying on our road.

Next, there are those more significant and definite perceptions, thoughts, feelings, volitions, which have a closer connection with our purposeful life. Here too we shall find that a very high proportion of them is in a state of utter confusion. Hundreds of crosscurrents flash through the mind, and everywhere there are "bits and ends" of unfinished thoughts, stifled emotions, passing moods. Many of them meet a premature death owing to their innate feeble nature, our lack of concentration, or through being suppressed by new and stronger impressions. If we observe our own mind, we shall notice how easily diverted our thoughts are, and how often they behave like undisciplined disputants constantly interrupting each other and refusing to listen to the other side's arguments. Again, many lines of thought remain rudimentary or are left untranslated into will and action, because courage is lacking to accept the practical, moral or intellectual consequences of these thoughts. If we continue to examine closer the reliability of our average perceptions, thoughts or judgments, we shall have to admit that many of them are just the products of habit, led by prejudices of intellect and emotion, by our pet preferences or aversions, by laziness and selfishness, by faulty or superficial observations, and so on.

Such a look into long-neglected quarters of the mind will come as a wholesome shock to the observer. It will convince him of the urgent need for methodical mental culture extending not only to a thin surface layer of the mind, but also to those vast twilight regions of consciousness to which we have paid now a brief visit. The observer will then become aware of the fact that a reliable standard of the inner strength and lucidity of consciousness in its totality cannot be derived from the relatively small sector of the mind that stands in the intense light of purposeful will and thought, nor can it be judged by a few optimal results of mental activity achieved in brief, intermittent periods. The decisive factor in determining the quality of individual consciousness is whether that dim awareness characteristic of our everyday mind and the uncontrolled portion of everyday activity tend to increase or decrease.

It is the daily little negligence in thoughts, words and

deeds going on for many years of our life (and as the Buddha teaches, for many existences) that is chiefly responsible for creating and tolerating that untidiness and confusion in our minds which we have described. The old Buddhist teachers said:

Negligence produces a lot of dirt and dust, even a whole heap of refuse. It is as if in a house only a very little dirt collects in a day or two; but if this goes on for many years, it will grow into a vast heap of refuse.

It is in the dark, untidy corners of the mind where our most dangerous enemies dwell. From there they attack us unawares, and much too often they succeed in defeating us. That twilight world peopled by frustrated desires and suppressed resentments, by vacillations and whims and many other shadowy figures, forms a background from which upsurging passions—greed and lust, hatred and anger—may derive powerful support. Besides, the obscure and obscuring nature of that twilight region is the very element and mother-soil of the third and strongest of the roots of evil *(akusala-mūla)*, i.e., ignorance or delusion.

Attempts at eliminating mind's main defilements—greed, hate and delusion—must fail as long as these defilements find refuge and support in these uncontrolled dim regions of the mind; as long as the close and complex tissue of those half-articulate thoughts and emotions forms the basic texture of mind into which just a few golden strands of noble and lucid thought are woven. But how to deal with that unwieldy, tangled mass? Man usually tries to ignore it, and to rely on the counteracting energies of his surface mind. But the only safe remedy is just to face it—with mindfulness. Nothing more difficult is needed than to acquire the habit of noticing these rudimentary thoughts as often as possible, i.e., to direct bare attention to them. The working principle here is the simple fact that there cannot exist two thoughts at the same time: if the clear light of mindfulness is present, there is no room for mental twilight. When sustained mindfulness has secured a firm foothold, it will be a matter of, comparatively, secondary importance in which ways the mind will then deal with those rudimentary thoughts, moods and emotions. It may just dismiss them and replace them by purposeful thoughts; or it may allow them, and even compel them, to complete what they have to say. In the latter case, they will often reveal how poor and weak they actually are; and it will then not be difficult to dispose of them, once they are forced into the open. This procedure of bare attention is very simple and effective; the difficulty here is only the persistence in applying it.

Observing a complex thing means identifying its component parts, singling out the separate strands forming that intricate tissue. If this is applied to the complex currents of mental and practical life, automatically a strong regulating influence will be noticeable. As if ashamed in the presence of the calmly observing eye, the course of thoughts will proceed in a less disorderly and wayward manner; it will not so easily be diverted and will resemble more and more a well-regulated river.

During decades of the present life and throughout millenniums of traversing the round of existence, there has been steadily growing within man a closely fitted system of instinctive and reflex actions (beneficial and harmful ones), of prejudices of intellect and emotions—in brief, of bodily and mental habits that are no longer questioned as to their rightful position and useful function in human life. Here again it is the application of bare attention that loosens the hard soil of these often very ancient layers of the human mind, preparing thus the ground for sowing the seed of methodical mental training. Bare attention identifies and pursues the single threads of that closely interwoven tissue of our habits. It sorts out carefully the subsequent justifications of passionate impulses and the pretended motives of our prejudices; it questions fearlessly old habits often grown meaningless, and by uncovering their roots it helps in abolishing all that is seen to be harmful. In brief, bare attention lays open the minute crevices in the seemingly impenetrable structure of unquestioned mental processes. Then the sword of wisdom wielded by the strong arm of constant meditative practice will be able to penetrate these crevices, and finally to break up that structure where it is required. If the inner connections between the single parts of a seemingly compact whole become intelligible, then it ceases to be inaccessible.

If the facts and details of its conditioned nature become known, there is a chance of effecting fundamental changes in it. In that way, not only those hitherto unquestioned habits of the mind, its twilight regions and its normal processes as well, but even those seemingly solid, indisputable facts of the world of matter—all of them will become "questionable" and lose much of their self-assurance. By that bland self-assurance of assumed "solid facts" many people are so impressed and intimidated that they are reluctant to take up any spiritual training, doubting that it can effect anything worthwhile at all. The results of applying bare attention to the task of tidying and regulating the mind will therefore greatly encourage those who are still hesitant to enter a spiritual path.

In conclusion, we wish to point out that the tidying or regulating function of bare attention is of fundamental importance for that "purification of beings" mentioned by the Buddha as the first aim of *satipatthāna*. It refers of course to the purification of their minds, and here the very first step is to bring an initial order into the way of functioning of the mental processes. We have seen how this is done by bare attention. In that sense, the Commentary to the Discourse on mindfulness explains the words "for the purification of beings" as follows:

It is said: 'Mental taints defile the beings; mental clarity *(citta-vodāna)* purifies them.' That mental clarity comes to be by this way of mindfulness *(satipatthāna-magga)*.

Naming
We have mentioned before that the tidying or regulat-

11

ing function of bare attention takes the form of sorting out and identifying the various confused strands of the mental process. That identifying function is, like any other mental activity, connected with a verbal formulation. In other words, "identifying" proceeds by way of expressly "naming" the respective mental processes.

There is an element of truth in the "word magic" of primitive men. "Things that could be named had lost their secret power over man, the horror of the unknown. To know the name of a force, a being or an object was [to primitive man] identical with the mastery over it."* That ancient belief in the magical power of "knowing the name" appears also in many fairy tales and myths where the power of a demon is broken just by facing him courageously and pronouncing his name.

In the practice of bare attention, one will find a confirmation of that power of naming. Particularly, the "demons of the twilight region" of the mind cannot bear the simple, but clarifying question about their "names," much less the knowledge of these names, which alone is often sufficient to diminish their strength. They cannot bear the calmly observing glance of the wanderer on the Buddha's way of mindfulness. That glance, however, has not the effect of driving them back into their hiding places, but it has, on the contrary, the magical power to force these demons of our passionate impulses and obscure thoughts into the open, into the daylight of consciousness. There they will feel embarrassed and obliged to justify themselves, though, at this stage of bare attention, they have not yet even been subjected to any closer questioning except that about their "names," their identity. If forced into the open, while still in an incipient stage, they will be incapable of withstanding scrutiny, and will just dwindle away. Thus a first victory over them may be won, even at an early stage of the practice.

The appearance in the mind of undesirable and ignoble thoughts, even if they are very fleeting and only half-articulate, is an unpleasant experience to one's self-esteem. Therefore such thoughts are often shoved aside, unattended and unopposed. Often, also, they are camouflaged by more pleasing and respectable labels which hide their true nature. Thoughts disposed of in either of these two ways will increase the accumulated power of ignoble tendencies in the subconscious. Furthermore, the procedure adopted will weaken one's will to resist the arising and the dominance of mental defilements, and it will strengthen the tendency to evade the issues. But by applying the simple method of clearly and honestly "naming," that is registering, any undesirable thoughts, these two harmful devices, ignoring and camouflaging, are excluded, and their detrimental consequences on the structure of subconsciousness and on our conscious mental effort are avoided.

Calling those ignoble thoughts, or one's shortcomings such as laziness, by their right names, will arouse in one's mind a growing inner resistance and even repugnance against them, which may well succeed in keeping them in check and finally eliminating them. Even if these undesirables are not fully brought under control by such means, they will carry with them the impact, that is, the recollection, of a repeated resistance against them, and this will weaken them in cases of their reappearance. If we may continue to personify them, we may say that they will no longer feel like unopposed masters of the scene, and this diffidence of theirs will make it considerably easier to deal with them. It is the power of moral shame *(hiri-bala)* that has been mustered here as an ally, and it is methodically strengthened by these simple, yet subtle psychological means.

The naming and registering extends of course also to noble thoughts and impulses which will be encouraged and strengthened by it. Without such deliberate attention to them, they may often pass unnoticed and remain barren, while a clear awareness of them will stimulate their growth.

It is one of the most beneficial features of right mindfulness, and in particular of bare attention, that it enables us to utilize for our progress all external events and all inner processes of mind. Even the unsalutary can be made a starting point for the salutary if, through the device of "naming" or "registering," it becomes an object of detached knowledge.

In several passages of the *Satipatthāna Sutra* the function of "naming" or "bare registering" seems to be indicated through formulating the respective statements by way of direct speech. There are not less than four such instances in the Discourse:

1. "When experiencing a pleasant feeling, he knows, 'I experience a pleasant feeling';

2. "He knows of a lustful [state of] mind, 'Mind is lustful';

3. "If [the hindrance of] sense desire is present in him, he knows, 'Sense desire is present in me';

4. "If the enlightenment factor mindfulness is present in him, he knows, 'The enlightenment factor mindfulness is present in me.' "

In conclusion, it may briefly be pointed out that the *tidying up* and the *naming* of mental processes is the indispensable preparation for fully understanding them in their true nature, which is the task of insight *(vipassāna)*. These functions, exercised by bare attention, will help in dispelling the illusion of compactness *(ghana-vinibbhoga)* of mental processes; they will also be helpful in tracing their specific nature or characteristics, and in noticing their momentary arising and disappearing.

The Noncoercive Procedure

Both the world surrounding us and the world of our own mind are full of unwanted experiences and frustrations, of hostile and conflicting forces. Man knows from his own bitter experience that he is not strong enough to meet and conquer in open combat each one of these antagonistic forces around him and within him. He knows that, in the external world, he "cannot have everything as he wants it," and that, in the inner world of his mind, passions and impulses, whims and fancies, are often victorious over the voices of duty, reason and higher aspirations.

Man knows further that often an undesirable situation will even worsen if excessive pressure is used against it. Thus passionate desires may grow in intensity if one tries to silence them by sheer force of will. Disputes and quarrels will go on endlessly and grow fiercer, if they are fanned again and again by angry retorts or by vain attempts to crush the other man's position entirely. A disturbance during work, rest or meditation, will be felt more strongly and will have a longer-lasting impact if one reacts to it by resentment, anger, or by attempts to suppress it.

Again and again man will meet with situations in life where he cannot *force* issues. But there are ways of mastering some of the vicissitudes of life and many of the conflicts of mind, without an application of force, by nonviolent means, which may often succeed where attempts of coercion, internal or external, have failed. Such a way of nonviolent mastery of life and of mind is *satipatthāna*. By the methodical application of bare attention, being the basic practice in the development of right mindfulness, all the latent powers of a noncoercive approach will gradually unfold themselves, with their beneficial results and their wide and unexpected implications. Here, in this context, however, we are mainly concerned with benefits for the mastery of mind and for progress in meditation that may result from a noncoercive procedure. But we shall also throw occasional side glances to the repercussions on everyday life. It will not be difficult for a thoughtful reader to make more detailed application to his own problems.

The antagonistic forces that appear in meditation, and are liable to upset its smooth course, are of three kinds:

1. external disturbances, such as noise;
2. mental defilements *(kilesa)*, including lust, anger, dissatisfaction, sloth, which may arise at any time during meditation; and
3. various incidental stray thoughts, or surrender to daydreaming.

The occurrence of these distractions is the great stumbling block for a beginner in meditation who has not yet acquired sufficient dexterity to deal with them effectively. To give thought to those disturbing factors only when they actually arise at the very time of meditation will be quite insufficient. If caught unprepared in one's defense, one will struggle with them in a more or less haphazard and ineffective way, and with a feeling of irritation which will form an additional impediment. If disturbances of any kind and an unskillful reaction to them occur several times during one session, one will feel utterly frustrated and irritated, and may have to give up further attempts at meditating, at least for the present occasion.

In fact, even meditators who are quite well informed, by books or teacher, about all details concerning the subject of meditation chosen, are often lacking in instruction how to deal skillfully with those varieties of disturbance mentioned above. The feeling of helplessness in the face of them is the most formidable initial difficulty for a beginner in meditation. Many have accepted defeat at that point, abandoning prematurely any further effort in methodical meditation. As in worldly affairs so in meditation, one's way of dealing with the "initial difficulties" will often be decisive for success or failure.

When faced by inner and outer disturbances, the inexperienced or uninstructed beginner will generally react in two ways: he will first try to shove them away lightly, and if he fails in that, he will try to suppress them by sheer force of will. But these disturbances are like insolent flies: by whisking—first lightly and then with increasing vigor and anger—one may succeed (or not) in driving them away for a while, but mostly they will return with an exasperating constancy, and the effort and vexation of "whisking" will have produced only an additional disturbance of one's composure.

Satipatthāna, through its method of bare attention, offers a nonviolent alternative to those futile and even harmful attempts at suppression by force.

A successful nonviolent procedure in mind control has to start with the right mental attitude. There must be first the full cognizance and sober acceptance of the fact that those three antagonistic forces or disturbing factors are co-inhabitants of the world we live in, whether we like it or not. Our disapproval of them will not alter the fact. With some of them we shall have to come to terms, and concerning others—the mental defilements—we have to learn how to deal with them effectively until they are finally conquered.

1. Since we are not the sole inhabitants of this densely populated world, there are bound to be *external disturbances* of various kinds, such as noise, interruption by visitors. We cannot always live in "splendid isolation," "from noise of men and dogs untroubled," or in "ivory towers" high above the crowd. Right meditation is not escapism; it is not meant for providing hiding places of temporary oblivion. Realistic meditation has the purpose of training man's mind to face, to understand and to conquer this very world in which we live and which also includes numerous obstacles to the life of meditation.

2. A *satipatthāna* master, the Venerable U Sobhana Mahāthera (Mahāsi Sayadaw) of Burma, said: "In an unliberated worlding *mental defilements* are sure to arise again and again. He has to face that fact, and he should know these defilements well, in order to apply again and again the appropriate remedy of *satipatthāna.* Then they will grow weaker, more short-lived, and will finally disappear." To know the occurrence and nature of defilements is therefore as important for a meditator as to know the occurrence of his noble thoughts.

By facing one's own defilements one will be stirred to increase the effort to eliminate them. On the other hand, by trying to avert one's glance when they arise, out of a false shame or pride, one will never truly join issue with them, and will always evade the final and decisive encounter; and by hitting blindly at them, one will only exhaust, or even hurt, oneself. But by observing carefully their nature and behavior when they arise in one's own mind, one will be able to meet them well prepared, to forestall them often, and finally to banish them fully. Therefore meet your defilements with a free and open glance! Be not ashamed, afraid or discouraged!

3. The third group of intruders disturbing the meditator's mind are the stray thoughts and daydreams which may consist of various memories and images of the recent or remote past, including those emerging from subconscious depths; thoughts of the future: planning, imagining, fearing, hoping; the casual sense perceptions that may occur at the very time of meditation, often dragging after them a long trail of associated ideas. Whenever concentration and mindfulness slacken, stray thoughts or daydreams will appear and fill the vacuum. Though they seem insignificant in themselves, they are, through their frequent occurrence, a most formidable obstacle, not only for the beginner, but in all cases when the mind is restless or distracted. Like the mental defilements, they will be entirely excluded only when, at the stage of holiness *(arahatta),* perfect mindfulness has been obtained, keeping unfailing watch at the door of the

mind. But it can certainly be achieved so that, even for long continuous periods of meditation, these invaders are kept at bay.

To all these facts about the three kinds of disturbing factors full weight must be given and the facts must be fully absorbed by our mind, if they are to shape our mental attitude. Then, in these three disturbing factors, the truth of suffering will manifest itself to the meditator very incisively through his own personal experience: "Not to obtain what one wants is suffering." Also the three other noble truths should be exemplified by reference to that very situation. In such a way, even when dealing with impediments, the meditator will be within the domain of *satipatthāna:* he will be engaged in the mindful awareness of the four noble truths, being a part of the contemplation of mental objects *(dharmānupassanā)*. It is a characteristic of right mindfulness, and one of its tasks, to relate the actual experiences of life to the truths of the *dharma*, and to use them as opportunities for its practical realization. Already here, at this preliminary stage devoted to the shaping of a correct and helpful mental attitude, we have the first successful test of our peaceful weapons: by understanding our adversaries better, we have consolidated our position, which was formerly weakened by an emotional approach; and by transforming these adversaries into teachers of the four noble truths, we have won the first advantage over them.

If mentally prepared by a realistic view of these three factors antagonistic to meditation, one will be less inclined to react at once by irritation when they actually arise. One will be emotionally in a better position to meet them with the nonviolent weapons of which we shall now speak.

There are three devices of countering disturbances which should be applied in succession whenever the preceding device has failed to dispose of the disturbance. All three are applications of bare attention, differing in the degree or intensity of attention given to the disturbance. The guiding rule here is: give no more mental emphasis to the respective disturbance than actually required by circumstances.

1. First, one should notice the disturbance clearly, but lightly; that is, without emphasis and without attention to details. After that brief act of noticing, one should try to return to the original object of meditation, and one may well succeed in it if the disturbance is weak by nature, or one's preceding concentration of mind was fairly strong. If, at that stage, we are careful not to get involved in any "conversation" or argument with the intruders, we shall, on our part, not give them a reason to stay long; and, in a good number of cases, the disturbances will depart soon, like visitors who do not receive a very warm welcome. That curt dismissal of them may often enable us to return to our original meditation without any serious disturbance to the composure of mind.

The nonviolent device is this: to apply bare attention to the disturbance, but with a minimum of response to it, and with a mind bent on withdrawal. This is the very way in which the Buddha himself dealt with inopportune visitors, as described in the *Mahāsunnata-Sutra:* ". . . with a mind bent on seclusion . . . and withdrawn, his conversation aiming at dismissing [those visitors]." Similar was Sāntideva's advice how to deal with fools: if one cannot avoid them, one should treat them "with the indifferent politeness of a gentleman."

2. If, however, the disturbance persists, one should repeat the application of bare attention again and again, patiently and calmly; and it may well be that the disturbance will vanish when it has spent its force. Here the attitude is: to meet the repeated occurrence of a disturbance by a reiterated "No," by a determined refusal to be deflected from one's course. It is the attitude of patience and firmness. The capacity of watchful observation has to be aided here by the capacity to wait and to hold one's ground.

These two devices will generally be successful with incidental stray thoughts, daydreams, etc., which are

feeble by nature; but also the other two types of disturbances, the external ones and defilements, may yield
quite often.

3. But if, for some reason or other, they do *not* yield,
one should now turn one's full and deliberate attention
to the respective disturbance, accept it as an object of
knowledge, and transform it thus from a *disturbance* of
meditation to a legitimate *object* of meditation. One may
continue with that new object until the external or internal cause for attending to it has ceased, or one may even
retain it for that session of meditation, if it proves satis-
factory.

If there is, for instance, disturbance by persistent
noise, we should give to it our undivided attention. But
we should take care to distinguish it well from any
reaction of ours concerning it, e.g., by resentment, which
likewise should be clearly recognized in its own nature,
whenever it arises. In doing so, we shall have undertaken
the contemplation of mind objects *(dharmānupassanā)*,
according to the following passage of the Discourse: "He
knows the ear and sounds, and the fetter (e.g., resentment) arising through both." If the noise is intermittent
or of varying intensity, one will be easily able to discern
the rise and fall *(udayabbaya)* in its process, and to add,
in that way, to one's direct insight into impermanency
(aniccatā).

The attitude towards recurrent mental defilements, as
thoughts of lust, restlessness, should be similar. One
should face them squarely, but distinguish them from
one's reaction to them, e.g., connivance, fear, resentment,
irritation. In doing so, one is making use of the device of
"naming," and one will reap its benefits which have been
outlined before. In the recurrent waves of passion or
restlessness one will likewise learn to distinguish gradually
phases of "high" and "low," their "ups and downs," and
may also gain other helpful knowledge about their behavior. By that procedure, one again remains entirely within
the range of *satipatthāna*, by practicing the contemplation of the state of mind *(cittānupassanā)* and of mind

objects *(dharmānupassanā;* i.e., attention to the hindrances).

This method of transforming disturbances of meditation into objects of meditation, as simple as it is ingenious, may be regarded as the culmination of nonviolent procedure. It is a device very characteristic of the spirit of *satipatthāna,* by making use of all experiences as aids on the path. In that way, enemies are turned into friends, because all these disturbances and antagonistic forces have become our teachers; and teachers, whoever they may be, should be regarded as friends.

We cannot forgo to quote here from a noteworthy little book, which is a moving human document of fortitude and practical wisdom acquired by suffering. It is *The Little Locksmith* by Katherine Butler Hathaway:

I am shocked by the ignorance and wastefulness with which persons who should know better throw away the things they do not like. They throw away experiences, people, marriages, situations, all sorts of things because they do not like them. If you throw away a thing, it is gone. Where you had something you have nothing. Your hands are empty, they have nothing to work on. Whereas, almost all those things which get thrown away are capable of being worked over by a little magic into just the opposite of what they were, . . . But most human beings never remember at all that in almost every bad situation there is the possibility of a transformation by which the undesirable may be changed into the desirable.

We have said before that the occurrence of the three disturbing elements cannot always be prevented. They are parts of our world, and their coming and going follows its own laws irrespective of our approval or disapproval. But by applying bare attention we can well prevent our being swept away or dislodged by them. By taking a firm and calm stand on the secure ground of mindfulness, we shall repeat in a modest degree, but in an essentially identical way, the historic situation under the *Bodhi* tree when

Māra, at the head of his army, claimed in vain possession of the soil on which the seat of enlightenment rested (as he will claim every inch of the world's surface). Trusting in the power of mindfulness, we may confidently repeat the Master's aspiration before his enlightenment: *Ma mam thānā acavayi!* May he *(Māra)* not dislodge me from this place" *(Padhāna Sutra)*.

Let the intruders come and go, like any other members of that vast, unceasing procession of mental and physical events that passes along before our observant eyes, in the practice of bare attention.

Our advantage here is the quite obvious fact that two thought moments cannot be present at one and the same time. Attention refers, strictly speaking, not to the present but to the moment that has just passed away. Thus, as long as mindfulness holds sway, there will be no "disturbance" or "defiled thought." This gives us the chance to hold on to that secure ground of an "observer's post," to the potential "throne of enlightenment."

By the quietening and neutralizing influence of detached observation as applied in our three devices, the interruptions of meditation will increasingly lose the sting of irritation, and, thereby, their disturbing effect. This will prove to be an act of true *virāga* ("dispassion"), which literally means "decoloring." That is to say, these experiences will lose their emotional tinge that excites towards lust and aversion, and they will appear as "bare phenomena" *(suddha-dharmā)*.

The nonviolent procedure of bare attention endows the mediator with a "light but sure touch" that is so essential for handling the sensitive, evasive and refractory nature of our mind, as well as for dealing with various difficult situations and obstacles in life. When speaking of the even quality of energy required for attaining to the meditative absorptions, the "path of purification" *(visuddhi-magga)* illustrates it by describing a test which the ancient students of the art of surgery had to undergo as a proof of their skill. A lotus leaf was placed in a bowl of water, and the pupil had to make in incision through

23

the length of the leaf, without cutting it entirely or submerging it. He who applied an excess of force either cut it into two or pressed it into the water, while the timid one did not even dare to scratch it. In fact, it is something like the gentle but firm hand of the surgeon that is required in mental training, and this skillful and well-balanced touch will be the natural outcome of the nonviolent procedure in the practice of bare attention.

For a full and unobstructed unfoldment of the mind's capacities, the influence of two complimentary forces is needed: *activating* and *restraining*. That twofold need was recognized by the Buddha, the great knower of mind. He advised that the faculties of energy *(viry'indriya)* and of tranquil concentration *(samādh'indriya)* should be kept equally strong and well balanced. Furthermore, he recommended three of the seven factors of enlightenment *(bojjhanga)* as suitable for rousing the mind,* and another three for calming it.** In both cases, among the spiritual faculties and the enlightenment factors, it is mindfulness *(sati)* that not only watches over their equilibrium, but actively stimulates the growth of their activating as well as their restraining power.

Mindfulness, though seemingly of a passive nature, is in fact also an activating force. It makes the mind alert, and alertness is indispensable for all purposeful activity. In the present inquiry, however, we shall be mainly concerned with the *restraining* power of mindfulness. We shall examine how it makes for disentanglement and detachment, and how it positively helps in the development of the mental qualities required for the work of deliverance.

In practicing bare attention, we *keep still* at the mental and spatial place of observation, amidst the loud demands of the inner and outer world. There is in it the strength of tranquility, the capacity of deferring action and applying the brake, of *stopping* rash interference, of suspending judgment while *pausing* for observation of facts and wise reflection on them. There is also a wholesome *slowing down* in the impetuosity of thought, speech and action.

Keeping still and stopping, pausing and slowing down—
these will be our key words when speaking now of the
restraining effect of bare attention.

An ancient Chinese book says: "In making things end,
and in making things start, there is nothing more glorious
than *keeping still.*"

In the light of the Buddha's teaching, the true "end of
things" is *nirvāna* which is called the *"stilling* of formations" *(sankhārānam vūpasamo)*, that is, their final end or
cessation. It is also called "the stopping" *(nirodha).* The
"things" or "formations" meant here are the conditioned
and impersonal phenomena rooted in their twofold cause,
craving and ignorance. The end of formations comes to
be by the end of "forming," i.e., by the end of world-
creating *karmic* activities. It is the "end of the world"
and of suffering, which, as proclaimed by the Buddha,
cannot be reached by walking, by migrating or transmi-
grating, but is to be found only within ourselves. That
"end of the world" is heralded by each deliberate act of
keeping still, stopping or *pausing.* "Keeping still," in that
highest sense, means: stopping the accumulation of
karma. It means refraining from perpetually adding to
our entanglements in *samsāra*, abstaining from our
unceasing concern with evanescent things. By following
the way of mindfulness, and training ourselves to keep
still, or pause, in the attitude of bare attention, we refuse
to take up the world's persistent challenge to our disposi-
tions for greed or hatred. We protect ourselves against
rash and delusive judgments; we refrain from blindly
plunging into the labyrinths of interfering action with all
its inherent dangers.

"He who abstains from interfering, is everywhere in
security."

(Sutra-nipāta, verse 953)

"He who keeps still [or: knows where to stop] will not
meet danger."

(Tao-Te-King, Chapter 44)

The Chinese saying, quoted earlier, says in its second part that there is nothing more glorious in *making things start* than keeping still. Explained in the Buddhist sense, these things effectively started by keeping still, are "the things [or qualities] making for decrease of *karmic* accumulation" *(apacayagāmino dharmā)*, and, in dealing with them, we may follow the traditional division of mental training into morality (or conduct), concentration (or tranquility) and wisdom (or insight). All three are decisively helped by the attitude of *keeping still,* as cultivated by bare attention.

1. *Conduct.* How can we improve our conduct, its moral quality and its skill in making right decisions? If we earnestly desire such an improvement, it will generally be the wisest to choose the line of least resistance. We might suffer discouraging defeat if we turn too early against those shortcomings which have deep roots in old habits or in powerful impulses. We shall be better advised to pay attention first to those blemishes of our actions or speech and to those errors of judgment which are caused by thoughtlessness and rashness, and there are many of them. There are numerous instances in the lives of most of us where one short moment of reflection may have prevented a false step, and thereby warded off a long chain of misery or moral guilt that started with a single moment of thoughtlessness. But how can we curb our rash reactions and replace them by moments of mindfulness and reflection? This will depend on our capacity to *stop and pause,* to apply the brakes at the right time, and that we can learn well by practicing bare attention. In that practice we shall train ourselves "to look and wait," to suspend, or slow down, reactions. We shall learn it "in the easy way," in situations of our own choice, within the limited field of experiences met with during the periods of meditative practice. When facing again and again the incidental sense impressions, feelings or stray thoughts which interrupt our concentration; when curbing again and again our desire to respond to them in some way or other; when succeeding again and again in keeping

still in face of them—then we shall be well prepared for preserving that inner stillness also in the wider and unprotected field of everyday life. We shall have acquired a presence of mind that will enable us to pause and stop, even if we are taken by surprise, or are suddenly provoked or tempted.

Our present remarks refer to those blemishes of conduct which are liable to arise through thoughtlessness and rashness, but might more or less easily be checked through mindfulness. Dexterity in dealing with them will, however, also affect those more obstinate deviations from moral conduct which are rooted in strong passionate impulses or in deeply ingrained bad habits. The increased tranquility of mind achieved in keeping still for bare attention will restrain the impetuosity of passions, and the acquired habit of "pausing and stopping" will act as a brake to the unquestioned repetition of bad habits.

By being able to keep still for bare attention, or to pause for wise reflection, very often the first temptation to lust, the first wave of anger, the first mist of delusion will disappear without causing serious entanglement. At which point the current of unwholesome thought processes is stopped will depend on the quality of mindfulness. If mindfulness is keen, it will succeed in calling a stop at a very early point of a series of defiled thoughts or actions, before we are carried too far along by them. Consequently, the respective defilements will not grow beyond their initial strength, less effort will be required to check them, and less *karmic* entanglements, or none, will follow.

Let us take the example of a pleasant visual object which has aroused our liking. At first that liking might not be very active and insistent. If here the mind is already able to keep still for detached observation or reflection, it will be easily possible to divest the visual perception of its still very slight admixture of lust, and to register it as "just something seen that has caused a pleasant feeling"; or the effect of the attraction felt is sublimated into quiet aesthetic pleasure. If that earliest chance has been missed, the liking will grow into attachment and into desire to possess. If now a stop is called, the thought of desire *(akusala-mano-karma,* "unwholesome mental *karma")* may express itself by speech *(akusala-vacl-karma,* "unwholesome verbal *karma"):* one will follow. But if the current of lust is still unchecked, the thought of desire *(akasala-mano-kamma,* "unwholesome mental *karma")* may express itself by speech *(akusala-vacl-kamma,* "unwholesome verbal *karma"):* one asks for the desired object, or even demands it with impetuous words. A refusal will cause the original current of lust to branch out into additional streams of mental defilements, either of sadness or of anger. But if even at that late stage one can stop for quiet reflection or bare attention and, accepting the refusal, renounce wish fulfilment, further complications will be avoided. But if clamoring words are followed by action *(akusala-kāya-karma,* "unwholesome bodily *karma"),* if, driven by craving, one tries to get possession of the object of one's desire by stealth or force, then the *karmic* entanglement is complete, and the full impact of its consequences will be experienced by the doer. Still, if even after the completion of the evil act, the doer stops for reflection, i.e., if mindfulness takes the form of remorseful retrospection, it will not be in vain: it will preclude a hardening of character and may prevent a repetition of the same course of action.

The exalted one said once to his son Rāhula:

Whatever action you *intend* to perform, by body, speech or mind, you should consider that action .... If, in considering it, you realize: 'This action which I intend to perform will be harmful to myself, or harmful to others, or harmful to both; it will be an unwholesome action, producing suffering, resulting in suffering'—then you should certainly not perform that action.

Also *while* you are performing an action, by body, speech or mind, you should consider that action .... If, in considering it, you realize: 'This action which I am performing is harmful to myself, or harmful to others, or harmful to both; it is an unwholesome action, producing suffering, resulting in suffering'—then you should desist from such an action.

Also *after* you have performed an action, by body, speech or mind, you should consider that action .... If, in considering it, you realize: 'This action which I have performed has been harmful to myself, or harmful to others, or harmful to both; it was an unwholesome action, producing suffering, resulting in suffering'—then you should in future refrain from it.

2. *Tranquility.* We shall now consider how the stopping for bare attention is also a helper in attaining or strengthening tranquility *(samatha)* in its double sense: of peace of mind in general, and of meditative concentration and calm.

By growing a habit of pausing and stopping for bare attention, it will become increasingly easier to withdraw into one's own stillness when unable to escape bodily from the loud and insistent noises of the outer world; it will be easier to forgo useless reaction to foolish speech or deeds of others. Also when the blows of fate are particularly hard and incessant, a mind trained in bare attention will find it easier to take refuge in the haven of apparent passivity, or watchful nonaction, and to wait patiently until the storms have passed. There are situations in life when it is best to allow things to come to their natural end. He who is able to keep still and wait will often succeed where aggressiveness or busy activity is vanquished. Not only in critical situations, but also in the normal course of life, the experience won by observant keeping still will convince us that it is not at all necessary to make an active response to every impression received, or to regard every encounter with people or things as a challenge to our interfering activity.

By refraining from busying ourselves unnecessarily, external frictions and, thereby, internal tensions will be reduced. Greater harmony and peace will pervade the life of every day, and the sometimes considerable contrast of normal life to the tranquility of meditation will be reduced. Then there will be less of those disturbing inner reverberations of everyday restlessness which, in a coarse or subtle form, invade the hours of meditation and produce bodily and mental unrest. Consequently, the hindrance of agitation *(uddhacca-nivarana)*, which is a chief obstacle of concentration, will be less often evident, or it will be easier to overcome it.

By cultivating the attitude of bare attention as often as opportunity offers, the centrifugal forces of mind, making for mental distraction, will be reduced, and the centripetal tendency, turning the mind inward and making for concentration, will be strengthened. The craving for a variety of changing objects of thought, or objects of desire, will be effectively checked.

Furthermore, regular practice of sustained attention to a continuous series of events will prepare for sustained concentration on a *single* object or a limited number of objects in the strict practice of meditation. Firmness, or steadiness, of mind, being another important factor in concentration, will likewise be cultivated in that way.

Thus, by keeping still, pausing and stopping for bare attention, several salient components of meditative tranquility are fostered: calmness, concentration, firmness, reduction of the multiplicity of objects. The average level of normal consciousness is raised and brought closer to the level of the meditative mind. This is an important point, because it happens often that too wide a gap between these two levels of mind will frustrate again and again attempts of mental concentration or the achieving of smooth continuity in meditative practice.

In the sequence of the seven factors of enlightenment we find that the enlightenment factor tranquility *(passadhi-sambojjhanga)* precedes that of concentration *(samādhi-sambojjhanga):* and, expressing the same fact, it was said, "If tranquilized within, the mind will become concentrated." Now, in the light of our previous remarks, we shall better understand these statements.

3. *Insight.* It has been said by the exalted one: "He whose mind is concentrated sees things as they really are." Therefore all those ways by which bare attention strengthens concentration of mind will also be a supporting condition of the development of insight. But there is also a more direct and specific help which insight receives from "keeping still at bare attention."

Apart from (supposedly) disinterested scholarly or scientific research, man is generally more concerned with "handling" and utilizing things, or defining their relations to himself, than with knowing them in their true nature. He is therefore mostly satisfied with registering the very first signal conveyed to him by an outer or inner perception. Through deeply ingrained habit, that first signal will evoke standard responses by way of judgments like good-bad, pleasant-unpleasant, useful-harmful, right-wrong; which again will lead to further reactions by word or deed in accordance with these judgments. It is very rare that attention will dwell any longer upon an object of a common, or habitual type, than for receiving that very first signal, or the first few. Thus, mostly only one single aspect of the object, or a selected few, will be perceived (and sometimes misconceived), and only the very first phase (or little more) of the object's life span will come into the focus of attention. One may not even be consciously aware that the respective process has an extension in time (origination and end); that it has many aspects and relations beyond those at first sight connected with the casual observer or the limited situation; that, in brief, it has a kind of evanescent individuality of its own. A world that has been perceived in that superficial way, will, to that extent, consist of rather shapeless little lumps of experiences marked by a few subjectively selected (and sometimes misapplied) signs or symbols which have significance mainly for the individual's self-interest. Parts of that rather shadowlike world are not only things and persons of one's environment, but even a good part of one's own bodily and mental processes which are often conceived in a similar superficial way. When thus the seal of self-reference is stamped again and again upon the world of every day experience, the basic misconception—"This belongs to me" *(attaniya)*—will steadily continue to grow subtle, but firm and widespread roots (comparable to the hair roots of plants), which will scarcely be shaken by mere intellectual convictions about the nonexistence of a self *(anattā)*.

These grave consequences issue from that fundamental perceptual situation we have mentioned: on receiving a first signal from his perceptions, man rushes into hasty or habitual reactions which so often commit him to the four misapprehensions of reality: taking the impure for pure, the impermanent for lasting, the painful and pain-bringing for pleasant, and the impersonal for a self or something belonging to the self.

But if one musters the restraining forces of one's mind and pauses for bare attention, the material and mental processes that form the objects of mind at the given moment will reveal themselves more fully and more truly. If they are no longer dragged at once into the whirlpool of self-reference, but allowed to unfold themselves before the watchful eye of mindfulness, the diversity of their aspects and the wide net of their correlations and interconnections will appear: the narrow and often falsifying connection with self-interest will recede into the background and will be dwarfed by the wider view now gained. Birth and death, rise and fall of many of the observed processes will be clearly discerned, in their serial occurrence or in their component parts. Thereby the facts of change and impermanence will impress themselves on the mind with growing intensity. By the same discernment of rise and fall, many false conceptions of unity in the processes which had been created under the influence of the egocentric attitude will be dissolved. Self-reference uncritically overrides diversity, and lumps things together under the preconceptions of *being* a self *(attā)* or *belonging* to a self *(attaniya)*. But bare attention reveals these sham unities as impersonal and conditioned phenomena. Facing thus again and again the evanescent, dependent and impersonal nature of life processes within and without, their monotony and unsatisfactory nature will become marked; in other words, the truth of suffering inherent in them will appear. In that way, all three characteristics, or signata, of existence will open themselves to penetrative insight *(vipassanā)*, by the simple device of slowing down, pausing and keeping still for bare attention.

Spontaneity

An acquired or strengthened habit of pausing mindfully before acting will not exclude or paralyze spontaneity of response where it is beneficial. On the contrary, the pausing, the stopping and the keeping still for bare attention will, through training, become quite spontaneous themselves. They will grow into a "selective mechanism" of the mind that, with an increasing reliability and swiftness of response, will prevent the upsurge of evil or unwise impulses which may have been intellectually realized by us as unwholesome, but, by their own powerful spontaneity, still continue to defeat our better knowledge and nobler intention. The practice of mindful pausing serves, therefore, to replace unwholesome spontaneity or habits by wholesome ones.

Just as certain reflex moments are an automatically operating protection of the body, similarly a spontaneously working spiritual and moral self-protection will be a vital function of the mind. A person of average moral standard will instinctively shrink from theft or murder, without any long reflection. With the help of the method of bare attention, the range of such spontaneously functioning moral brakes can be greatly extended and ethical sensitivity heightened. Also false thought habits can be broken in the same way and replaced by correct ones.

In an untrained mind, noble tendencies or right thoughts often succumb to the spontaneous outbreak of passions or prejudices, or they can assert themselves only with difficulty, after a struggle of motives. But if the spontaneity of the unwholesome is checked or greatly reduced, as described above, our good impulses and wise reflections will have greater scope and they will be able to express themselves freely and spontaneously. Their spontaneous flow will give greater confidence in the power of the good within us and will carry more conviction for others. That spontaneity of the good will not be of an erratic nature, but will have deep and firm roots in previous methodical training. Here appears a way by which the "premeditated good" *(sasankhārika-kusala)* may be transformed into "spontaneously arising good thought" *(asankhārika-kusala-citta)* which, if combined with knowledge, takes the first place in the scale of ethical values, according to the psychology of the *abhidharma.* Hereby we shall get practical understanding of a saying in *The Secret of the Golden Flower:* "If one attains intentionally to an unintentional state one has comprehension." This saying just invites a paraphrase in Pāli terms: *Sasankhārena asankhārikam pattabbam,* "By premeditated intentional effort spontaneity can be won."

If the numerous aids to mental growth and liberation, found in the Buddha's teachings, are wisely utilized, there is actually nothing that can finally withstand the *satipatthāna* method; and this method starts with the simple, but in its effects far-reaching, practice of learning to pause and stop for bare attention.

Slowing down

Against the impetuosity, rashness and heedlessness of the untrained mind, practice of pausing and stopping sets a deliberate slowing down. The demands of modern life, however, make it impracticable to introduce such a slow-down of functions into the routine of the average working day. But as an antidote against the harmful consequences of the hectic speed of modern life, it is all the more important to cultivate that practice in one's leisure hours and especially in periods of strict *satipatthāna* practice. It will also give the worldly benefits of greater calm, efficiency and skill in one's daily round of work.

For the purposes of meditative development, slowing down serves as an effective training in heedfulness, sense control and concentration. But apart from that, it has also more specific significance for meditative practice. In the commentary to the *Satipatthāna Sutra*, for instance, it is told how the slowing down of movements may help in *regaining lost concentration* on a chosen object. A monk, so we read, had bent his arm quickly without remembering his subject of meditation, as his rule of practice demanded. On becoming aware of that omission, he took his arm back to its previous position and repeated the movement mindfully. The subject of meditation referred to was probably "clearly comprehending action" *(sampajāna-kāra)*, and especially the one mentioned in the *Satipatthāna Sutra* as follows: "In bending and stretching he acts with clear comprehension" *(Samminjite pasārite sampajānakāri hoti)*.

The slowing down of certain bodily movements during strict meditative training is also of great help in gaining *insight knowledge (vipassanā-nāna)* by one's own experience, and especially the direct awareness of change *(anicca)* and impersonality *(anattā)*. It is, to a great extent, the rapidity of movement that strengthens the illusion of unity, identity and substantiality of what is actually a complex and evanescent process. Therefore, in the strict practice of *satipatthāna*, the slowing down of walking or bending and stretching and thereby discerning the several phases of each movement, is an exercise very helpful for direct insight into the three characteristics of all phenomena. It will make an impression of increasing force and significance on the meditator, to notice clearly how each partial phase of the process observed arises and ceases by itself, and nothing of it "goes over" or "transmigrates" to the next phase.

Also the average rhythm of our everyday actions, speech and thoughts will become more quiet and peaceful under the influence of that practice. Slowing down the hurried rhythm of life means that thoughts, feelings and perceptions will be able to complete the entire length of their natural lifetime. Full awareness will extend up to their end phase: to their last gentle vibrations and reverberations. Too often that end phase is cut off by an impatient grasping at new impressions, or by hurrying on to the next stage of a line of thought before the earlier one has been clearly comprehended. This is one of the main reasons for the disorderly state of average consciousness which is burdened by a vast amount of indistinct or fragmentary perceptions, of stunned emotions and unfinished or undigested ideas. Slowing down will prove an effective device for recovering the fullness and clarity of consciousness. A fitting simile, and at the same time an actual example of it, is the procedure in the practice of mindfulness on breathing *(ānāpānasati)* where mindfulness has likewise to cover the whole extent of the breath, its beginning, middle and end. This is what is meant by the passage of the Discourse, saying "Experiencing the *whole* (breath-)body, I shall breathe in and out." Similarly, the entire "breath," or rhythm, of our life will become deeper and fuller, if, through slowing down, we get used to sustained attention.

The habit of prematurely cutting off processes of thought, or slurring over them, has assumed serious proportions in the man of modern city civilization. His restlessness clamors for ever new stimuli, in an ever-increasing speed of succession, having its counterpart in the increasing speed of our means of locomotion. This rapid bombardment of impressions will gradually blunt man's sensitivity, and consequently the new stimuli will have to be still more loud, coarse and variegated—a process which, if not checked, can only end in disaster. This state of affairs also explains the decrease of finer aesthetic susceptibility and the growing incapacity of genuine natural joy. The place of both is taken by a hectic, short-breathed excitement which does not leave any true aesthetic or emotional satisfaction. "Shallow mental breath" is to a great extent responsible for the growing superficiality and coarseness of "civilized man" and for the frightening spread of nervous disorders in the West. It may well become the start of a general deterioration of human consciousness in its qualitative level, its range and its strength. This danger threatens all those, in the East as well as in the West, whom the impact of technical civilization finds without an adequate spiritual protection. *Satipatthāna* can make an important contribution to remedying that situation, in the way we have indicated here briefly. Thus, also from the worldly point of view, the method will prove beneficial.

Here, however, we are chiefly concerned with the psychological aspects and their significance for meditative development. Sustained attention, being helped by *slowing down*, will affect the quality of consciousness mainly in three ways: (a) the intensity of consciousness, (b) the clarity of the object's characteristic features, and (c) it will reveal the object's "relatedness."

(a) An object of *sustained* attention will exert a particularly strong and long-lasting impact on the mind, not only throughout the thought series immediately following the respective perception, but its influence may also extend far into the future. It is that causal efficacy which is the measure of the *intensity of consciousness.*

(b) The first impression conveyed by any new sense object or idea will be what is most striking in it, subjectively or objectively, and it will dominate the mind up to the culminating point of the impact. But there are sure to be other aspects, characteristics or functions of the respective object which may not be obvious or are less interesting to the cognizing subject but which are no less, or even more, important. There will also be cases where the first impression is entirely deceptive. Only if attention is sustained beyond that first impact will the respective object reveal itself more fully. It is only at the downward course of the first perceptual wave (its end phase), when the prejudicing force of the first impact lessens, that the object will yield a wider selection of detail, an all-around picture of itself. It is, therefore, only by sustained attention that a greater *clarity of an object's characteristic features* can be obtained.

(c) Among the characteristic features of a physical or mental object there is one class which is often overlooked by hasty or superficial attention, and therefore we list it here separately: it is the *relatedness* of the object, extending to its past (origin, causes, reasons, logical precedents, etc.), and its present manifestation (environment, "background," presently active influences, etc.). An event cannot be said to be fully understood, if it is viewed in artificial isolation. It must be seen as a part of a wider pattern, in its conditioned and conditioning nature; and this can be done only with the help of sustained attention.

The influence of slowing down and sustained attention on subconsciousness, memory and intuition

It need hardly be pointed out how important all these three aforementioned points are for "seeing things according to reality," in other words, for the development of insight *(vipassanā)*. Their *direct* influence is obvious, but there is also an *indirect* one which is no less powerful and important. Those three results of sustained attention, achieved with the help of *slowing down,* are also instrumental in influencing the quality and nature of *subconsciousness, memory* and *intuition* which, on their part, will again be aiding, nourishing and consolidating the progress of liberating insight. Insight aided by them will be like the mountain lake (of the canonical simile) that is fed not only from without, by the rains, but also by springs welling up within its own depth. Similarly, insight will be nourished not only through external experience but also from the "subterraneous," i.e., subliminal resources of the mind: by memories, other subconscious material, and by the strengthened faculty of intuition. Meditative results of an insight that has such deep roots will not be lost easily, even with unliberated worldlings *(puthujjana)* who are subject to relapse.

1. If perceptions or thoughts which have been objects of sustained attention sink into *subconsciousness,* they will occupy there a special position by reason of their

stronger impact on the mind and the greater distinctness of their characteristic features. As to the first reason: it will certainly not remain without any effect upon the structure of subconsciousness, if the end phase of a moment of consciousness or of a cognitive series, being immediately followed by subconsciousness, is not weak but of a strength equal to that of the preceding phases. As for the second reason: if an impression or idea, marked by numerous and distinct characteristics, sinks into subconsciousness, it will not so easily be absorbed into the vagueness of other subconscious contents or dragged into false subconscious associations with superficial similarities of passionate biases. And also the last of the aforementioned three facts—the correct comprehension of the object's "relatedness"—will have similar effects: there will be a greater resistance against a merging with inadequate subconscious material. If perceptions or thoughts of that level of intensity and clarity sink into subconsciousness, they will be more "articulate" and more "accessible" than contents of subconsciousness originating from hazy or "stunned" impressions; they will be more easily "convertible" into full consciousness, and less unaccountable in their hidden effects upon it. If, through an improvement in the quality and range of mindfulness, the number of such "matured" impressions increases in the mind, it seems quite possible that a subtle change in the structure of subconsciousness can be achieved in that way.

2. It will be evident from our earlier remarks that those impressions which we have called "matured" or "more easily accessible and convertible," will lend themselves more easily and more correctly to recollection. More easily, because of their greater intensity; more correctly, because of their clearly marked features which will give them a fair degree of protection against being distorted by false associative images or ideas. If, in addition, they are remembered in their "context" and "relatedness," it will work both ways, for easier and more correct recollection. In that way, *sati*, in its meaning and function

of mindfulness, will help to strengthen *sati* in its meaning and function of memory.

3. From that very influence on subconsciousness and memory also a deepening and strengthening of the faculty of intuition will naturally follow, and particularly of, intuitive insight, which concerns us here chiefly. Intuition is not a "a gift from the unknown," but, as any other mental faculty, it arises out of specific conditions which, in this case, are primarily the latent memories of perceptions and thoughts "stored" in the subconscious. It is obvious that memories which have the aforementioned qualities of greater intensity, clarity and richness of distinctive marks, and thereby of greater accessibility, will provide the most fertile soil for the growth of intuition. Here too the preserved "relatedness" of the respective impressions will contribute much. Recollections of that type will have a more organic character than memories of bare or vague, isolated facts, and they will more easily fall into new patterns of meanings and significance. These more "articulate" memory images will be a strong stimulation and aid for the intuitive faculty. Silently and in the hidden depths of the subliminal mental processes, the work of collecting and organizing the subconscious material of experience and knowledge goes on until it is ripe to emerge, as what we call an *intuition*. The breaking through of that intuition is sometimes occasioned by quite ordinary happenings which, however, may have a strong evocative power, if, in previous occurrence they had been made objects of sustained attention. Slowing down and pausing for bare attention will reveal the depth dimension of the simple things of every day, and will thus provide potential stimuli for the intuitive faculty. This applies also to the intuitive penetration *(pativedha)* of the four noble truths that culminates in holiness *(arahatta)*. Many instances are recorded of monks where the flash of intuitive penetration did not strike them when they were engaged in the meditative practice of insight proper, but on quite different occasions: when stumbling, when seeing a forest fire, a fata morgana, a lump of froth in a river.

We have met here another confirmation of that seemingly paradoxical saying that "intentionally" an unintentional state may be won, or at least aided, by deliberately turning the full light of mindfulness even on the smallest events and actions of everyday life.

Sustained attention not only provides the nourishing soil for the *growth* of intuition, it also makes possible the fuller utilization and even repetition of the intuitive moment. Men of inspiration in various fields of creative activity have often related and deplored their common experience that the flash of intuition strikes so suddenly and vanishes so quickly that frequently the slow response of the mind scarcely catches the last glimpse of it. But if the mind has been trained in observant pausing, in slowing down and sustained attention, and if—as indicated above—also the subconsciousness has been influenced by it, then the intuitive moment, too, might gain that fuller, slower and stronger rhythm. This being the case, its impact will be strong and clear enough for making full use of that flash of intuitive insight. It might even be possible to lead its fading vibrations upward again to a new culmination, similar to the rhythmic repetition of a melody rising again, in harmonious development, out of the last notes of its first appearance.

The full utilization of a single moment of intuitive insight might be of decisive importance for one's progress toward full realization. If one's mental grip is too weak and those elusive moments of intuitive insight are allowed to slip away without being utilized fully for the work of liberation, then it might well happen that they will not recur before many years have passed, or perhaps not at all during the present life. Skill in sustained attention, however, will allow the full use of opportunities, and slowing down and pausing during meditative practice is an important aid in acquiring that skill.

Through our now-concluded treatment of pausing, stopping and slowing down, one of the traditional definitions of mindfulness found in the Pali Scriptures will have become more intelligible in its far-reaching implications:

that is, its function of *anapilāpanatā*, meaning literally, "not floating (or slipping) away," "like pumpkin pots on the surface of water," add the commentators; and they continue: "Mindfulness enters deeply into its object," instead of hurrying over its surface only. Therefore "non-superficiality" will be an appropriate rendering of the above Pali term, and a befitting characterization of mindfulness.

Directness of Vision

*I wish I could disaccustom myself from everything,
so that I might see anew, hear anew, feel anew.*

G. Chr. Lichtenberg (1742-1799)

In an earlier section, we spoke about the impulsive spontaneity of the unwholesome *(akusala)*. We have seen how the stopping for bare and sustained attention is able to counter, or reduce, the occurrence of rash impulsive reactions, thus allowing us to face any situation with a fresh mind, with *a directness of vision*, unprejudiced by those first spontaneous responses.

By *directness of vision* we understand a direct view of reality, without any coloring or distorting lenses, without the intrusion of emotional or habitual prejudication and intellectual biases. It means coming face to face with the bare facts of actuality, seeing them as vivid and fresh as if they had occurred for the first time.

The force of habit

Spontaneous reactions, which so often stand in the way of direct vision, do not derive only from passionate impulses, but are very frequently the product of *habit;* and, in that form, they generally have an even stronger and more tenacious hold on man, which may work out either for the good and useful or for the bad and harmful. The influence for the *good* exercised by habit is seen in the "power of repeated practice" by which man's achievements and skills, of a manual or mental, worldly or spiritual kind, are protected against loss or forgetfulness, and are converted from a casual short-lived and imperfect acquisition into the more secure possession of a quality thoroughly mastered. The *detrimental* effect of habitual, spontaneous reactions is manifest in what is called, in a derogative sense, the "force of habit": its deadening, stultifying and narrowing influence, productive of compulsive behavior of various kinds. In our present context, we shall be concerned only with that negative aspect of habit as impeding and obscuring the directness of vision.

As remarked earlier, the influence of habitual reactions is generally stronger than that of impulsive ones. Passionate impulses may disappear as suddenly as they have arisen. Though their consequences may well be very grave and extend far into the future, it is mostly the influence of habit which is longer lasting and deeper reaching. Habit spreads its vast and closely meshed net over wide areas of our life and thought, trying to drag in more and more of it. Passionate impulses too, might be caught into that net of habit and thus be transformed from passing outbursts into traits of character. A momentary impulse, an occasional indulgence, a passing whim may by repetition become a habit difficult to uproot, a desire hard to control, and finally an automatic function that is no longer questioned. By repeated gratification of a desire, habit is formed, and habit grows into a compulsion.

It may well be the case that some activity, behavior or mental attitude to which one has become accustomed is, considered by itself, quite unimportant to the individual concerned, and also morally quite indifferent or inconsequential. At the start it might have been quite easy to abandon it or even to exchange it for its very opposite, since neither one's emotions nor reason had any strong bias towards either side of a possible choice. But by repetition, the continuance of the chosen way of acting, behaving or thinking will gradually become equivalent with "pleasant," "desirable," "correct" or even "righteous"; and it will be finally identified, more or less consciously, with one's so-called character or personality. Consequently, any change in it—a break in that routine— will be felt as "unpleasant" or as "wrong," and any interference with it from outside will be greatly resented and even regarded as hostile towards "one's vital interests and principles." In fact, primitive minds, at all times, be they "civilized" or not, have looked at a stranger with his "stranger customs" as an enemy, and have felt his mere unaggressive existence as a challenge or threat to themselves.

In the cases aforementioned, when the specific habit was originally not of great importance to the individual, the attachment which is gradually formed is not so much to the object proper, as to the pleasantness of undisturbed routine. The strength of that attachment to routine derives partly from the force of physical and mental inertia which is so powerful in man. About another cause of it we shall speak presently. By force of habit, the respective concern (any material object, activity, behavior or way of thinking) is invested with such an increase of emotional emphasis that the attachment to quite unimportant or banal things may become as tenacious as that to the fundamental passions in man. Thus, even the smallest habits, if, by lack of conscious control they become uncontested masters of their respective realms, may dangerously contribute to the rigidity and self-limitation of character, narrowing its "freedom of movement" (environmental, intellectual and spiritual). Thus, often quite unnecessarily, new fetters are forged for the individual, and nourishing soil is provided for the growth of new attachments and aversions, prejudices and predilections, that is to say, for new suffering. Therefore, when considering the following words of the *Satipatthāna Sutra*, we should also think of the important part played by habit in the formation of fetters:

> ... and what fetter arises dependent on both [i.e., the sense organs and sense objects], that he knows well. In what manner the arising of the not-arisen fetter comes to be, that he knows well.

In Buddhist parlance, it is preeminently the hindrance of sloth and torpor *(thīna-middha-nivarana)* which is strengthened by the "force of habit," and mental faculties like agility and pliancy of mind *(kāya-* and *citta-lahutā, mudutā)* are weakened.

The danger for spiritual development, involved in the dominating influence of habit, is all the more serious since its tendency towards expansion is particularly noticeable in our present age of increasing specialization and standardization in various spheres of life and thought.

The roots of that tendency of habits to extend their range are anchored in the very nature of consciousness. Certain active types of consciousness, if possessing a fair degree of intensity, tend to repeat themselves, though that tendency is never quite undisputed, e.g., by new cognitions claiming man-attention. This tendency towards repetition stems not only from the aforementioned passive force of inertia, but in many cases from an active "will to dominate and to conquer." Even in quite peripheral or subordinate types of consciousness, there seems to exist an urge to gain ascendancy, to become by themselves ever so small centers around which other, weaker mental and physical states revolve, adapting themselves to that center and becoming subservient to it. This is a striking parallel to the self-assertion and the domineering tendency of an egocentric individual in his contact with society. Among biological analogies, we may mention the tendency towards expansion by cancer and other pathological growths; and for the tendency towards repetition, we may think of the freak mutations which loom as a grave danger at the horizon of our atomic age.

Out of that "will to dominate," inherent in many types of consciousness, a passing whim may grow into a relatively constant trait of character, and, if still not satisfied with its position, it may tend to break away entirely from the present combination of life forces till, finally, in the process of rebirths, it becomes the very center of a new so-called personality. There are within us countless seeds for new lives, for innumerable potential "beings," all of which we should vow to liberate from the wheel of *samsāra,* as the Sixth Zen Patriarch expressed it.

Detrimental physical or mental habits may grow strong, not only if fostered deliberately, but also if left unnoticed or unopposed. From minute seeds planted in a long-forgotten past, has grown much of what has now strong roots in our nature. This growth of morally bad or otherwise detrimental habits can be effectively checked by gradually developing another habit that will counter them: that of attending to them mindfully. Doing deliberately what had become a mechanical performance, and, perhaps, previous to it, pausing for a while for bare attention and reflection—this will give a chance for scrutinizing the habit in the light of clear comprehension of purpose, and of suitability *(sātthaka-* and *sappāya-sampajanna)*. It will allow a fresh assessment of the situation, a *direct vision* of it, unobscured by the mental haze surrounding a habitual activity, which conveys the feeling: "It is right because it was done before." Even if a detrimental habit cannot be broken at once, or soon, in that way, it will still lose a good deal of its unquestioned spontaneity of occurrence; it will carry the stamp of repeated scrutiny and resistance, and at its reoccurrence it will be weaker and prove more amenable to our attempts to change or abolish it.

It needs hardly to be mentioned that habit (which was rightly called "the wet-nurse of man") cannot and should not disappear from our life. Let us only remember what a relief it is, particularly in the crowded day and complex life of a city dweller, that he can do a great number of things fairly mechanically, with, as it were, only "half-powered attention." It means a considerable simplification of his life. It would be an unbearable strain, if all that had to be done with deliberate effort and close attention. In fact, many products of manual labor, much of the *technique* in art, and even standard procedure in complex intellectual work, will generally bring better and more even results through skilled routine performance. Yet, also, that evenness of habitual performance will reach its dead point where it declines. It will show symptoms of fatigue if it is not enlivened by the creation of new interest in it.

There is, of course, no question of our advocating here the abolishment of all our little habits as far as they are innocuous or even useful. But we should regularly convince ourselves whether we have still control over them, that is, whether we can give them up, or alter them, whenever wanted. We can make sure of it, firstly, by attending to them mindfully for a certain period of time, and secondly, by actually giving them up temporarily in cases where this will not have any harmful or disturbing effects upon ourselves or others. If we turn on them the light of *direct vision*, looking at them or performing them as if seen or done for the first time, these little routine activities, and the habitual sights around us, will assume a new glow of interest and stimulation. This holds good also for our professional occupation and its environment, and for our close human relationships if they should have become stale by habit. The relations to one's marriage partner, to friends, colleagues, may thus receive a great rejuvenation. A fresh and direct vision will also reveal that one can react to people, or do things, in a different and more beneficial way than done before, habitually.

An acquired capacity to give up *little* habits will prove its worth in the fight against more dangerous proclivities, and also at times when we are faced with serious changes in our life which by force deprive us of very fundamental habits. Loosening the hardened soil of our routine behavior and thoughts will have an enlivening effect on our vital energy, our mental vigor, our power of imagination, and, what is most important, into that loosened soil we shall be able to plant the seeds of vigorous spiritual progress.

Associative thought

Mental habituation to standard reactions, to sequences of activity, to judgments of people or things, proceeds by way of associative thinking. From things or ideas, situations or people that we encounter, we select certain of their distinctive characteristics or marks, and associate, i.e., connect these marks with our own response to them. If these encounters recur, they are associated first with those marks selected earlier, and then with our original, or strongest, response, so that these marks become a signal for releasing a standard reaction which may consist of quite a long sequence of connected acts or thoughts, well-mastered or known through repeated practice of experience. That way of functioning relieves man of the necessity to apply ever-renewed effort and painstaking scrutiny to each single step of such sequences of thought and action. This certainly means a great simplification of life and a release of energy for other tasks. In fact, in the evolution of the human mind, associative thinking has been a progressive step of decisive importance. It was indispensable for acquiring the capacity to learn from experience, and led up to the discovery and application of causal laws.

Yet, it is easy to see that, close to these benefits of associative thinking, there lurk as many and grave dangers in this, now basic, procedure of mental activity, if it is faultily applied or not carefully watched. Let us draw up a list of these danger points (though not an exhaustive one):

1. Initial faulty or incomplete observations, errors of judgment, emotional prejudices (love, hate, pride), may be easily perpetuated and strengthened by the mechanism of associative thinking, through being carried over to reoccurrences of similar situations.

2. Incomplete observations and restricted viewpoints in judgments, which may have been sufficient for meeting a particular situation, may, if mechanically applied to changed circumstances, prove quite inadequate and may entail grave consequences.

3. Not infrequent are cases where, by misdirected associative thinking, a strong instinctive dislike is felt for things, places or persons which, in some way, are merely reminiscent of unpleasant experiences.

These briefly-stated instances show how vital it is to scrutinize from time to time these mental grooves of our associative thoughts, and the various habits and stereotype reactions deriving from them. In other words, we must step out of the ruts for a while, regain a direct vision of things and make a fresh appraisal of them in the light of that vision.

If we look once again over the list of potential dangers deriving from uncontrolled associative thinking, we shall better understand the Buddha's insistence on getting to the bedrock of experience. For instance, in the profound and terse stanzas called "The Cave," included in the *Sutra Nipāta*, he says that the "full penetration of *sense impression (phassa)* will make one free from greed" and that "by understanding *perception (sannā)* one will be able to cross the flood of *samsāra.*" By placing mindfulness, as a guard, at the very first gate through which experience enters, we shall be able to control the incomers much more easily, and shut out unwanted intruders. Thus the purity of "luminous consciousness" can be maintained against "adventitious defilements."

The *Satipatthāna Sutra* provides a systematic training for inducing direct, fresh and undistorted vision, covering the entire personality in its physical and mental aspects, and including the entire world of experience. The methodical application of the several exercises to oneself *(ajjhatta)*, to others *(bahiddhā)* and alternatingly to both, will be very helpful in discovering false conceptions due to misdirected associative thinking or misapplied analogies.

The principal types of false associative thinking are covered, in the terminology of the *dharma*, by the four kinds of *misapprehensions* or *perverted views (vipallāsa)* which wrongly take (1) what is impermanent, for permanent, (2) what is painful, or conducive to it, for happiness, (3) what is not-self and unsubstantial, for a self or an abiding substance, and (4) what is impure, for beautiful. These perverted views of reality arise through a one-sided and incomplete selection, or entirely false apprehension, of the characteristic marks of things or ideas, and through "associating" them closely with one's passions and false theories. By gradually "dissociating" our perceptions and impressions from these misapprehensions, with the help of bare attention, we shall make steady progress in the *direct vision* of "bare processes" *(suddha-dharmā)*.

The sense of urgency (samvega)

He who is being stirred *(samvijja)* to a sense of urgency *(samvega)* by things which are deeply moving to one of clear and direct vision, will experience a release of energy and courage that is able to break through his timid hesitations and his rigid routine of life and thought. If that sense of urgency is kept alive, it will bestow the earnestness and persistence *(appamāda)* required for the work of liberation.

Thus said the teachers of old:

This very world here is our field of action.
It harbors the unfoldment of the holy path,
And many things to break complacency.
Be stirred by things which may well move the heart.
And being stirred strive wisely and fight on!

Ayam kammabhūmi, idha maggabhāvanā,
thānāni samve janiyā bahu idha,
Samvega samve janiyesu vatthūsu,
samvega jāto 'va payunja yoniso.

Our nearest neighborhood is full of stirring things, but generally we do not perceive them as such, because habit has made our vision dull and our heart insensitive. Even the Buddha's teaching which, when we first encountered it consciously, was a powerful intellectual and emotional stimulation, will gradually lose for us its original freshness and impelling force, unless we constantly renew it by turning to the fullness of life around us which illustrates the four noble truths in ever new variations. A direct vision will impart new lifeblood even to the commonest experiences of every day, so that their true nature appears through the dim haze of habit, and speaks to us with a fresh voice. It may well be just the long accustomed sight of the beggar at the street corner, or a weeping child or the illness of a friend, which startles us afresh, makes us think, and stirs our sense of urgency in treading resolutely the path that leads to the cessation of suffering.

We know the beautiful old account of Prince Siddhartha's coming face to face with old age, illness and death, when he drove in his chariot through the paternal city, after a long time of isolation in a makebelieve world. This ancient story may well be historical fact, because we know that in the lives of many great ones often events occur which gain a symbolic significance or have great consequences far beyond their ordinary appearances. Great minds find significance in the seemingly common and invest with a far-reaching efficacy the fleeting moment. But, without conflicting with the inner truth of that old story, it may well have happened that the young prince had actually seen before, with his fleshly eye, old and sick people and those who had succumbed to death. But, on all these earlier occasions, it may not have touched him very deeply—as it is the case with most of us, most of the time. That earlier lack of sensitivity may have been due to the carefully protected, artificial seclusion of his petty (though princely) happiness into which his father—by the hereditary routine of his life—had placed him. Only when he broke through that golden cage of easygoing habits, the facts of suffering struck him as forcibly as if he had seen them for the first time. Then only was he stirred by them to a sense of urgency that led him out of the home life and set his feet firmly on the road to enlightenment.

The more *clearly* and *deeply* our minds and hearts respond to the truth of suffering as appearing in the very common facts of our existence, the less often we shall need a repetition of the lesson learned, the shorter will be our migration through *samsāra*. The *clarity* of perception evoking our response will come from an undeflected directness of vision, bestowed by bare attention *(sati);* and the *depth* of experience will come from wise reflection or clear comprehension *(sampajanna).*

The road to insight

Directness of vision is also a chief characteristic of the methodical practice of insight meditation *(vipassanā-bhāvanā).* There it is identified with the direct or experiential knowledge *(paccakkha-nāna)* bestowed by meditation, as distinguished from the inferential knowledge *(anumāna-nāna)* obtained by study and reflection. In the meditative development of insight, one's own physical and mental processes are directly viewed, without the interference of abstract concepts or the filtering screens of emotional evaluation, which, in this context, will only obscure, or camouflage, the naked facts, and detract from the immediate strong impact of reality. Conceptual generalizations interrupt the meditative practice of bare attention, tend to "shove aside," or dispose of, the respective particular fact, by saying, as it were: "It is nothing else but . . ." Generalizing thought inclines to become impatient with a recurrent type, and finds it soon boring after having it classified. Bare attention, however, being the key instrument of methodical insight, keeps to the particular. It follows keenly the rise and fall of successive physical and mental processes, and though all phenomena of a given series may be "true to type" (e.g., inhalations and exhalations), bare attention regards each of them as a distinct "individual," and conscientiously registers, as it were, its separate birth and death. If mindfulness remains alert, these repetitions of type will, by their multiplication, exert not a reduced but an intensified impact on the mind. The three signata or characteristics (change, misery and voidness) inherent in the process observed will stand out more and more clearly, appearing in the light shed by the phenomena themselves, and not in a *borrowed* light (borrowed not even from the Buddha, though he is the peerless and indispensable guide to these experiences).

These physical and mental phenomena, in their "self-luminosity," will then convey a growing sense of urgency to the meditator: revulsion, dissatisfaction, awareness of danger will arise concerning them, followed by detachment—though, certainly, joy, happiness and calm, too, will not be absent throughout the practice. Then, if all other conditions of inner maturity are fulfilled, the first direct vision of final liberation will dawn, with the stream-winner's *(sotāpanna)* indubitable knowledge: "Whatever has the nature of arising, has the nature of vanishing."

Thus, in the unfoldment of the fourfold power of mindfulness, *satipatthāna* will prove itself as the true embodiment of the *dharma* of which it was said:

Well proclaimed is the *dharma* by the Blessed One, visible here and now, not delayed, inviting of inspection, onward leading, and directly experiencable by the wise.

The Unity Press Mindfulness Series publishes in finely designed, quality paperback editions, commentaries on the Satipatthana and related eastern and western mindfulness exercises. This continuing series will be comprised of books of the highest insight transmitted to Unity Press via the meditations and psychic investigations of authorities of the highest accomplishment. Included are books offered to Unity Press by the Buddhist Publishing Society of Ceylon.

Presently available in the Unity Press Mindfulness Series are:

> *The Satipatthana Vipassana Meditation* By The Venerable Mahasi Sayadaw.
> A basic mindfulness exercise given monks upon entering the monastery. $1.75

> *Practical Insight Meditation* By The Venerable Mahasi Sayadaw.
> An advanced investigation of the basic and progressive stages of the power of consciousness to break through to the reality that lies beyond. $2.25

> *The Power Of Mindfulness* By The Honorable N. Thera.
> An inquiry into the scope of Bare Attention and the principle sources of its strength. $2.25